SOUTHFIELD PRIMARY SCHOOL
SOUTHFIELD ROAD
BEDFORD PARK
LONDON W4 1BD

Sandwiches

LYNN HUGGINS-COOPER

A & C Black • London

Published 2007 by A & C Black Publishers Limited
38 Soho Square, London W1D 3HB
www.acblack.com

Hardback ISBN: 978-0-7136-7108-7
Paperback ISBN: 978-0-7136-7686-0

Editor: Sarah Gay
Designer: Miranda Snow

The author and publishers would like to thank Clare Benson and Sue Dutson for
their advice in producing this series of books.

A CIP catalogue record for this book is available from the British Library.

Printed and bound in Singapore by Tien Wah Press (PTE) Limited.

Picture credits: front cover(br), Foodcollection/Getty; front cover(bl), 17, 20, 24(t), 25,
Peter Titmuss/Alamy; back cover, 11, LOOK Die Bildagentur der Fotografen
GmbH/Alamy; 4, Roy McMahon/Corbis; 5, Photolibrary.com/Getty; 6,
Bettmann/Corbis; 7, Ronen Zvulun /Reuters/Corbis; 8, Michael Brauner/Getty; 10,
Envision/Corbis; 12, Matthew Klein/Corbis; 13, Henry Romero/Reuters/Corbis ; 14,
24(b), Richard Price/Getty; 15, 24(m), Adam Woolfitt/Corbis; 16, BananaStock/Alamy;
18, foodfolio/Alamy; 19, James Leynse/Corbis; 22(tl), Annie Griffiths Belt/Corbis; 22(tr),
Tim Hall/Getty; 22(bl), Kathy deWitt/Alamy ; 22(br), Glenn Glasser/zefa/Corbis; 23(tl),
Ric Ergenbright/Corbis; 23(tr), Jenny Acheson/Getty; 23(bl), Matt Henry
Gunther/Getty; 23(br), Joe McBride/Getty.

Contents

Words printed in **bold** can be found in the glossary.

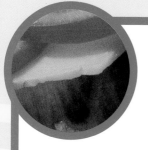

What are sandwiches?

Sandwiches are the ideal snack food for people on the move. They are great to take on trips or to school for lunch because they are quick to make and easy to eat. They can be made at home, or bought from shops and cafés everywhere.

A sandwich is usually thought of as two slices of bread with a filling between them, but there are hundreds of different kinds of sandwich. Open sandwiches, wraps, butties and *paninis* are all types of sandwich. They all use different kinds of bread to hold a filling. Some sandwiches are raw, some are cooked, some are sweet and some savoury, some are hot and some are cold.

▼ Open sandwiches are often eaten in Denmark. Only one slice of bread is used and the filling is placed on top.

A sandwich can be a ▶ very satisfying snack.

Sandwiches in history

The first sandwich was eaten over 2000 years ago! A Jewish leader called Hillel the Elder put a mixture of chopped nuts, apples, spices and wine between two pieces of flat bread, called *matzahs*. This became a Jewish tradition at Passover.

Modern sandwiches are named after John Montagu, the fourth Earl of Sandwich. He liked to play cards, and in 1762 he started to put his meat and cheese between two slices of bread so that he could eat it all with one hand while he carried on playing. The bread also stopped his hands getting dirty and kept his cards clean. Seeing this, other players asked for "the same as Sandwich"!

John Montagu, the fourth Earl of Sandwich

FACT!

When the Hawaiian islands were first discovered in 1778, Captain James Cook named them the Sandwich Islands after the Fourth Earl of Sandwich, who was his superior officer.

These Jewish girls are making *matzahs* for the Passover festival. ▷

Good for you!

Sandwiches make a good lunchtime meal because they are quick and easy to eat, and they can give us a mixture of foods from the five food groups.

Bread gives us energy to work and play. Fillings can be made from layers of meat, fish, cheese, salad, and all sorts of other foods. It is important to use healthy fillings which will give our bodies what they need to grow and to work properly throughout the day.

The 'balanced plate' diagram on page 9 shows some foods from the five food groups that we need to eat to stay healthy.

FACT!

The British Sandwich Association says that more and more people are thinking about staying healthy. Bread made from whole wheat is the healthiest kind of bread, and seeds and grains make bread healthier too. More healthy sandwiches with low fat fillings, such as salad and lean meat, are being sold every year.

▼ This healthy bread roll is covered in pumpkin seeds.

Eating lots of fruit and vegetables keeps our bodies working properly.

We should eat plenty of bread, cereals and potatoes to give us energy.

Dairy foods such as butter, cheese, eggs and milk help to keep our bones strong.

Eating too many fatty and sugary foods is bad for us.

Meat, fish and beans help our bodies to grow and repair themselves.

Try it out!
DESIGN A HEALTHY SANDWICH

1 Think about what kind of bread would make the sandwich healthy.

2 Use a variety of healthy ingredients as fillings.

Lean meat, fish, nuts or **Quorn** could provide the **protein** we need for our bodies to grow and repair themselves. Salad or vegetables could provide the **vitamins** we need to stay healthy.

Sandwiches around the world

Different kinds of sandwich can be found all over the world. The kinds of bread and fillings used depend on what foods are available locally and the flavours people enjoy in each country.

In France, people eat a hot sandwich called a *croque monsieur*. It is a cheese and ham sandwich with the crusts cut off, which is grilled or fried in butter.

Mexican *burritos* are made from a soft, flat bread that looks like a pancake. The bread is filled with beans, meat or fish, spicy salsa and sour cream, then rolled up so the filling is folded inside.

In Israel, fried balls made of beans or chickpeas called *falafel* are stuffed inside a pitta bread with salad.

Sandwiches from countries all around the world are now sold in shops and cafés across the UK. There are hundreds of different tastes and **textures** to try.

▲ Pitta bread is shaped like a pocket and the falafel are put inside.

F A C T !
In the UK, each person eats around 155 sandwiches a year on average. The British Sandwich Association says that around 2432 million sandwiches are sold in shops and cafés every year!

Try it out!
LOOK AT A RANGE OF PACKAGED SANDWICHES TRADITIONAL TO DIFFERENT COUNTRIES

1 Open the sandwiches, have a taste and take them apart. Are they fresh? What texture does the bread have?

2 What fillings and spreads have been used? Is there enough filling in the sandwiches?

3 **Evaluate** the sandwiches and decide which ones would be best as part of a 'healthy option'.

A Mexican lady ▶ makes lots of different Mexican sandwiches like *burritos, fajitas* and *tacos* to sell.

Super sandwiches!

Sandwiches can be all sorts of shapes and sizes. Some sandwiches are so big that you have to eat them with a knife and fork!

The club sandwich is a double-decker sandwich made from three slices of toasted, white bread. The bottom layer is usually crammed with ham, turkey or chicken, and the top layer is filled with bacon. It is often so big that it needs a cocktail stick to hold it together.

A *calzone* is a cross between a pizza and a sandwich. Pizza dough is stuffed with cheese, different meats and vegetables, and cooked until the dough bakes and the filling is hot. It looks like a big, fat, folded-over pizza.

The world's largest sandwich was made in the USA in 2005. It was 3.6 metres long and 3.6 metres wide, and was filled with mustard, corned beef, cheese and lettuce.

◀ Club sandwiches were first made in America.

This giant sandwich was made in Mexico in 2004. It was filled with ham, cheese and lettuce.

Try it out!
DESIGN A FILLING FOR YOUR OWN CALZONE

1 Have a go at making your own *calzone* with some ready-made pizza bases.

2 Think of all the different kinds of cheese, meat and vegetables you could use, and which toppings taste good on pizza.

Ask an adult to help you. Always remember to wash your hands before you start handling food.

All kinds of bread

The most important part of any sandwich is the bread. Without it you would have nothing to hold the filling in!

Bread is usually made with flour, water and yeast. Sometimes extra ingredients are added to change the flavour or texture of the bread. Yeast helps bread to rise by creating air bubbles in the dough, which make it **expand**. Pitta bread, *matzah* and *chapatis* are all flat because they are made without using yeast.

▼ All these types of bread were made using yeast. How many different types of bread can you see?

Try it out!
CARRY OUT A SURVEY TO FIND OUT WHICH TYPES OF BREAD YOUR FAMILY AND FRIENDS PREFER

1 Think about how you are going to collect and present the information in your survey.

2 Select five different types of bread. Offer people a taste of each type of bread, and ask them to rank them in order from 1 (their favourite) to 5 (their least favourite).

3 If possible, put the information onto a computer and make a database.

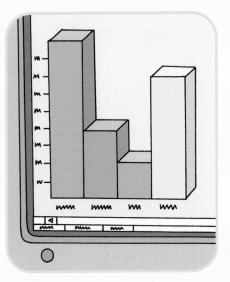

4 Create a graph of your results.

These bread rolls have been made into the shape of hedgehogs! ▶

Hedgehogs £1·25

Baby Hedgehog 60p

Sandwich fillings

Fillings are what make sandwiches tasty! Sandwiches can be made from any combination of fillings you can think of.

FACT!

The British Sandwich Association carried out a survey to find out which sandwiches people prefer. They found that unflavoured chicken sandwiches were the best seller, followed by ham, tuna, bacon, flavoured chicken, egg and then prawn.

Butter, margarine or mayonnaise is usually spread onto the bread before adding the filling to a sandwich. They help to stop sandwiches from being too dry, and they add to the flavour. They also help to stop moist fillings making the bread go soggy.

Sandwich fillings can be savoury, such as meat, cheese, salad or vegetables. They can also be sweet, like jam, honey, chocolate spread or fruit. Some sandwiches use both savoury and sweet fillings, such as cheese and pickle or the American favourite, peanut butter and jam.

◄ These children are filling sandwiches with peanut butter and jam.

These sandwiches are filled with (from the top) cheese and salad; sausage, egg and bacon; cream cheese and roasted peppers with lettuce; prawn cocktail with salad.

Try it out!

DESIGN THREE SANDWICH FILLINGS FOR A PICNIC WITH YOUR FRIENDS

1 Try to think of tasty but healthy fillings that contain ingredients from different food groups (see page 9).

2 Think about sauces or spreads you could add to the sandwich so that it is tasty and not too dry. Don't make it too wet or sloppy and make a mess!

Making sandwiches safely

The kitchen can be a dangerous place. There are lots of things you need to think about to keep safe when you're working with food.

Hygiene is always important when preparing food. If you are not careful, **bacteria** that can be found on your hands, work surfaces and even on food can make you very ill. Before making sandwiches you

▲ When using a knife, always keep your fingers well away from the blade edge.

should always make sure that your hands, **utensils** and work surfaces are clean. Always be very careful when using sharp knives.

Some sandwich fillings like meat, eggs and soft cheese can cause food poisoning if they are stored at the wrong temperature or for too long. It is important to make sure all of your ingredients are fresh. Keep your sandwiches in the fridge until you are ready to eat them. Aluminium foil will help to keep them fresh in your lunchbox.

Some people are **allergic** to certain foods, like nuts or eggs, and these foods can be very dangerous to them. If you're making a sandwich for someone, always ask whether they have any allergies and make absolutely sure there are no traces of foods they are allergic to in the sandwich.

Try it out!
FIND OUT HOW TO STORE SANDWICHES SAFELY

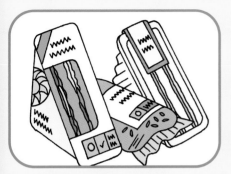

1 Look at pre-prepared sandwiches on sale in shops. Where are the sandwiches kept? Why do you think they are kept there?

2 What materials are used for the packaging? Why do you think these materials were chosen?

3 Write a report about your findings. Do you think the sandwiches were stored in the best way to keep them fresh?

Sandwiches ▶ in shops should always be kept in a refrigerator, and should be clearly labelled with a 'use by' date.

Technology solves problems!

Sometimes, people need to make lots of sandwiches all at the same time to sell in shops or cafés. Lots of sandwiches may be needed for a big party or a picnic. Making lots of sandwiches at once can take a very long time – unless technology is used to make things easier!

Making a big pile of cheese salad sandwiches involves slicing lots of bread, buttering, chopping salad and slicing cheese, which all takes a lot of time. If the bread was ready-sliced by a machine at the bakery, technology would be saving time and effort. Slicing the salad and cheese with a food processor would make things even quicker.

In factories, technology is used to make large numbers of sandwiches quickly and **efficiently**. When a large job is broken down into smaller parts, it is called a production line. The different parts of the job can be done by different people or machines.

◄ These production line workers are filling sandwiches with ham and salad.

Try it out!
MAKE YOUR OWN PRODUCTION LINE!

1 With a group of friends, make your own production line to produce a plate of sandwiches. Think about what bread and fillings you will use.

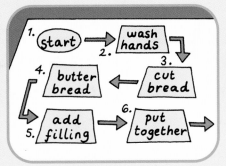

2 How many jobs will there be? Who will do which jobs? Plan every part of the job in the correct order, from buttering the bread to ending with a well-presented plate of sandwiches.

3 Now put it all into practice! Remember to work as a team and listen to each other.

4 Is there anything you could have done to make your production line work better?

Making sandwiches with a group of people can get very busy. Make sure you are organised so that you don't get in each other's way. Remember to always be careful around people who are using knives and make sure you don't distract them.

Sandwiches everywhere!

Sandwiches are enjoyed all over the world, in many different shapes and forms. They can be bought in all kinds of different places. Where do you buy yours?

A Jewish boy eats *falafel* in Jerusalem, Israel.

Sandwiches made with French bread are sold on the streets of Vietnam.

A man enjoys a sandwich from a market in London.

This man tucks into a bagel at a New York diner.

▲ A girl enjoys a wrap she made with her mother in their garden.

▲ This girl is making flat bread called *chapatis* in India.

▲ These boys are having fun making sandwiches in their kitchen in the Caribbean.

▲ This boy grabbed a quick sandwich for lunch at an amusement park in Australia.

Make your own...

DESIGN AND MAKE SANDWICHES FOR A BIRTHDAY PARTY

Imagine you are planning a birthday party with a dinosaur theme for your friends. Think of three different sandwiches to make for the party.

How can you find out what flavours your friends would enjoy?

Think about the different ways you could make the sandwiches look like dinosaurs. Will you use cutters, or a template, or add decorations to the sandwiches?

What sort of bread will you use? It will need to be soft enough to cut easily if you choose a cutter, but it must not be crumbly or your shapes will fall apart!

What fillings will you use? Remember to check whether any of your friends have food allergies. Draw exploded diagrams of

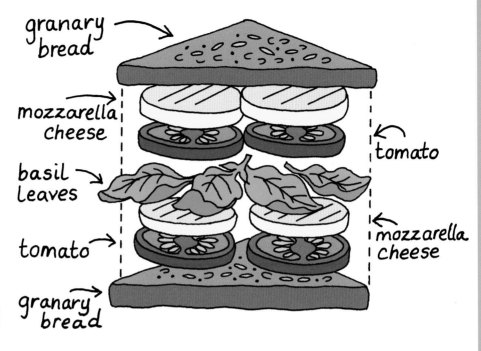

granary bread

mozzarella cheese

basil leaves

tomato

granary bread

tomato

mozzarella cheese

your sandwiches and describe how they can be made.

You might find it useful to make **prototypes** of your designs. Will you work with a team or alone to make the sandwiches?

Ask people to try the sandwiches and give you feedback about

the shapes and the taste and texture of the fillings and the bread. When you have had your feedback, decide which sandwiches you are going to make.

Brilliant books and wonderful websites

There are lots of great books and websites to help you learn more about sandwiches. When you are using the Internet, never give out details of your age or where you live, and make sure your parents and carers have a look at the websites you are visiting. They may learn something too!

BOOKS

Carla's Sandwich by Debbie Herman (Flashlight Press, 2004) – A story about a girl who loves experimenting with weird and wonderful sandwich fillings

I Can Do It! I Can Make a Sandwich by Susan Ashley (Gareth Stevens Publishing, 2004)

Sandwiches by Nicki Saltis (Sagebrush, 2001)

Super Sandwiches by Peter Sloan and Sheryl Sloan (Sagebrush, 2001)

Super Sandwiches: Wrap 'Em, Stack 'Em, Stuff 'Em by Rose Dunningham, (Lark Books, 2007)

Welcome Books: Let's Make a Sandwich by Mary Hill (Children's Press, 2002)

WEBSITES

www.sandwich.org.uk
The Home of the British Sandwich association online

www.warburtons.co.uk/recipe_ideas/kids.html
Lots of sandwich ideas for kids from the Warburtons website

www.iliveonyourvisits.com/sp/
Sandwich recipe ideas from the sandwich project

www.hovisbakery.co.uk
More sandwich ideas from the Hovis website

Glossary

allergic   when people's bodies are sensitive to certain things and they cause a bad reaction, like a rash or vomiting

bacteria   tiny living things which live all over the Earth and in the bodies of people and animals

efficiently   without wasting time or energy

evaluate   judge what you have done and decide if anything could be done better

expand   get bigger

food groups   all foods belong to one of five groups; we need to make sure that we eat foods from all five groups to stay healthy

hygiene   keeping clean to stay healthy and avoid illnesses

locally   in the area around where someone lives

Passover   a Jewish festival which celebrates the Israelites' escape from Egypt

protein   a substance found in some foods like meat or beans, which helps our bodies to grow and repair themselves

prototype   a first version of what you are going to make, which you can improve or base your final version on

Quorn   a vegetarian food made from tofu which is used to replace meat

texture   the feel of something

utensil   something used to prepare food in the kitchen

vitamins   natural substances found in foods that help our bodies to work properly

Index

Numbers in **bold** denote a picture.